THE POETRY WITCH
LITTLE BOOK
OF
WITCH POEMS

THE POETRY WITCH LITTLE BOOK OF WITCH POEMS

BY ANNIE FINCH

POETRY WITCH PRESS

Poetry Witch Press
Brooklyn, NY, USA
www.anniefinch.com

Book design by Sophia Renda

978-1-966557-00-5

POET'S NOTE

A poem is a spell, spun at the intersection of magic, word, and world. These poems spun themselves in my mind's ear, spiraling the patterns of their sounds down through my body. The sounds on their words drew me on, like the fragrance on flowers. Will you spiral these words through you as they came to me? Then say them aloud; speak them thrice; find the touch of their fragrances on your will, mind, body, heart, and spirit.

CONTENTS

BAUBO'S DANCE

Between my legs there is a mind
Before before and after after.

Join me here and you will find
Root and roar and wild laughter.

Join me here and we'll learn blind.
Faster. Slower. Slower. Faster.

Faster. Slower. Slower. Faster.
Long before and after after,

Join me here and you will find
Root and roar and wild laughter.

Join me here in the unwinding —
Faster. Slower. Slower. Faster.

Spin with me — and Spin with me —
and Spin with me and you will find

Between my legs there is a mind
Before before and after after.

BINDING SPELL

He who wastes a woman's will
Burns in flames that will never still.

He who mocks a woman's mind
Will be ruined by the wind.

He who abuses a woman's body
Mother Earth won't feed nor bury.

He who hurts a woman's heart
Rots where tears and oceans start.

He who scorns a woman's spirit
Loses his own birth within it.

FLOWER WHO WATERS ME

Trust me with growing too; how still I am,
Flower who opens my heart to run cool,
Trusting the rain, and the earth and the stem,

Cupped by the blossoms that bend without shame.
Flower who waters me, open my will;
Trust me with growing, too. How still I am.

Here comes a petal, as strong as a gem,
Guiding me down to where starlight meets soil,
Trusting the rain and the earth. And the stem —

Healing the touches I can overcome,
Flower who waters me, watches me wild,
Trust me with growing, too. How still I am:

Moving, I send my seeds. They are not tame;
Fertile, they're rooting to ring out a bell,
Trusting the rain, and the earth. And the stem —

Time-tongued and velvet and rough-cornered calm
Turning to, turning from — shattered, all full.
Trust me. With growing, too, how still I am,
Trusting the rain, and the earth. And the stem —

HEALING GREEN WATER SPELL

*Repeat three times aloud for healing

Green is the color that we travel in,
Moving through openings, never unbound
(After all, violet is only its skin).

Green sings the sound as the water comes in
Silent with openings, always (like sound's
Wild singing wings that close into the water).

Will we be ready, and will we be found,
There, in the depths, where tongues have been wound?
Green, after all, is the touch of the water,

I BURN WITH MY MOTHER, THE WITCH

For Maggie Finch, April 20, 1921 - January 14, 2018

I dreamed we were walking
        in fields that were green— all
the heartbreaking — beauty —
        of green — rearranging —
surrounded by men —
        were you mother, or sister? —

Our wrists roped together —
        our shaven heads — hanging —
We've loved through that bowing-down
        grass— (its long whisper—)
its — seed-heavy singing
        — or clanging, or changing —

Through so many lives —
        Now you're hearing Her call
Again — through the musk
        and the smoke — as I blister —
And bend —through the hope
        — of these embers — and crawl

KETTLE COVE

Through the upper and lower worlds, body and soul,
Through your softness and hardness, your wetness and roil,
May I rock in your mystery, speaking and whole,
Like the rockweeds You rock in your undersea coil!

You are fire in the rock and the water and wind,
in the earth and the sun and the ocean and air.

Like the rockweeds You rock in your undersea coil,
Half way between water and earth, I divide.
May I rock in your mystery, speaking and whole —
On your softness and hardness and wildness I ride!

In the center of sunlight, I am coming true!
In the pulling of ripples, I'm there!
I will answer your heart with me, my heart with You,
In this balance of waiting and air.

I am fire in the rock and the water and wind,
and the earth and the sun and the ocean and air.

On the point of the spray and the push of the tide,
I have rocked in your mystery, speaking and whole!
On your softness and hardness and wildness I ride
Like the rockweeds You rock, in your undersea coil!

NO SNAKE

Inside my Eden I can find no snake.
There's not one I could look to and believe,
obey and then be ruined by and leave
because of, bearing children and an ache.

I circle down on Eden from above,
searching the fields in solitude and love
like a high hawk. He would never forsake

this place that's made again of memory;
he'd wait in that tree below me, spring
out towards my growing shadow, let it bring
a sudden hope that he could coil free;

but he's not here. Only mountains that curve,
and dip around the valley when I swerve,
settle with dark heights, as I near the tree.

THE DOOR

It seemed as if a door came calling,
in a voice as old as carols,
telling lies as old as candles,
in words that were all about
some afternoons, lost on a child,
that could have been simple but
were lost, when I was just a child.

There was a day and then a dream
that I went through, and a cathedral
whose tall choir prayed
a singing message through the nave
until I heard a forest there
(though far outside, the trees were bare)

THE SPIRAL'S AT HAND

My sisters, we're burning —
but not in that fire!
The spiral's at hand —
where — we love, rule, and flower
Our world into life. It's

our time to inspire —
My sisters! We're burning!
But not in that fire —
Our witchy souls fly — home —
to truth and desire,

Turning at last —
in — our own sacred power —
My sisters. We're burning.
But not in that fire!
The spiral's at hand —
where we gather — and flower —

THE WOMAN ON THE BEACH

for Wallace Stevens

She could cliff and order waves, if they were climb-
ing up to reach her touch, or curling in
with drowning, freezing, fingers... She hears

the phantoms tooling over shale, their long
unrooting waverings singing the air
into her hands. Then, as she plants and pours,
learning her music, with no difference how

she seeds them out, or harvests in, or racks
the dark with her questioning, she pulls the caves
from sleep with her answering chant and noticing shore.
The waves won't hear her now; she won't feed them;

and it won't matter how she pulls them in,
gathers their green in seedlings weighted all
spiralling through, to make her bounded dream.

WITCHES

Fire and air and water and land.
Power grows where witches stand.

Power above, power below.
Witches shall find high and low.

Witches shall believe in earth.
Birth in body. Darker birth.

Power before and matrix after.
Witches shall believe in laughter.

Birth in spirit. Center. Love.
Witches shall believe and move.

WALK WITH ME

Walk with me just a while, body of sunlight,
body of grass, surface of trees,
head bending to the earth we have tasted,
body of death, surface of leaves.
Sinking hooves in the mud by the river,
root of the live earth, live through my body.
Sinking body, walk in me now.

ACKNOWLEDGEMENTS

"Baubo's Dance," first published in *Hobart Journal*

"Binding Spell," first published in *Nasty Women Poets: An Unapologetic Anthology of Subversive Verse*. Ed. Grace Bauer and Julie Kane, Lost Horse Press

"Healing Green Water Spell," first published in *Cimarron Review*

"Kettle Cove," first published in *Ecopoetry*

"No Snake," first published in *Eve* (Story Line Press, 1997)

"The Door," first published in *Eve* (Story Line Press, 1997)

"The Spiral's at Hand," first published in *Luna Luna*

"The Woman on the Beach," first collected in *Calendars* (Tupelo Press, 2003)

"Witches," first published in *Prairie Schooner*

"Walk With Me," first published in *Eve* (Story Line Press, 1997)

ABOUT THE POET

Annie Finch is the author of seven volumes of poetry, including *Calendars* and *Eve*, both finalists for the National Poetry Series, and *Spells: New and Selected Poems* (Wesleyan University Press). Her poetry has been featured in periodicals such as the *New York Times, Poetry Magazine,* and *The Paris Review* and books such as *The Penguin Book of Twentieth-Century American Poetry, Penguin Book of the Sonnet,* and *Norton Anthology of World Literature*. Finch is also the author of *A Poet's Craft: A Comprehensive Guide to Making and Sharing Your Poetry* and editor of ten anthologies including *A Formal Feeling Comes, Villanelles, An Exaltation of Forms, Measure for Measure: An Anthology of Poetic Meters,* and *Choice Words: Writers on Abortion*. Her other works include prosody, essays on poetics, poetry translation, and collaborations with choral music, opera, theater, and dance. Finch's work has been a finalist for the Yale Series of Younger Poets and Foreword Book Award and honored with the Arlt Prize, Sarasvati Award, and Robert Fitzgerald Award. She earned a Ph.D from Stanford University and served for a decade as Director of the Stonecoast MFA Program in Creative Writing. She is based in New York City and offers workshops and performances worldwide. For more information, please visit anniefinch.com